Riding on a Range

Western Activities for Kids

LAWSON DRINKARD

Illustrated by Fran Lee

Gibbs Smith, Publisher
Salt Lake City

First Edition

07 06 05 04 03   5 4 3 2 1

Text © 2003 by G. Lawson Drinkard III
Illustrations © 2003 by Fran Lee

Published by
Gibbs Smith, Publisher
P.O. Box 667
Layton, Utah 84041

www.gibbs-smith.com
Orders: 1-800-748-5439

Printed and bound in Hong Kong

Library of Congress Cataloging-in-Publication Data

Drinkard, G. Lawson, 1951–
Riding on a range : western activities for kids / Lawson Drinkard ;
illustrated by Fran Lee.—1st ed.
p. cm.
Summary: Provides information about what life is like for cowboys today, as well as in the past, introduces cowboy lingo and poetry, and gives ideas for how to experience some aspects of cowboy life.
ISBN 1-58685-036-9
1. Cowboys—West (U.S.)—Study and teaching—Activity programs—Juvenile literature. 2. Ranch life—West (U.S.)—Study and teaching—Activity programs—Juvenile literature. 3. West (U.S.)—Social life and customs—Study and teaching—Activity programs—Juvenile literature. [1. Cowboys—West (U.S.) 2. Ranch life—West (U.S.) 3. West (U.S.)—Social life and customs.] I. Lee, Fran, ill. II. Title.
F596 .D74 2003
636.2′13′0978—dc21
2002013190

For Sarah and Suzanne—
the cowgirls of my life.
— LD

For Jane, Karen, Mary, and Susan—
Yippee-Yay!
—FL

Contents

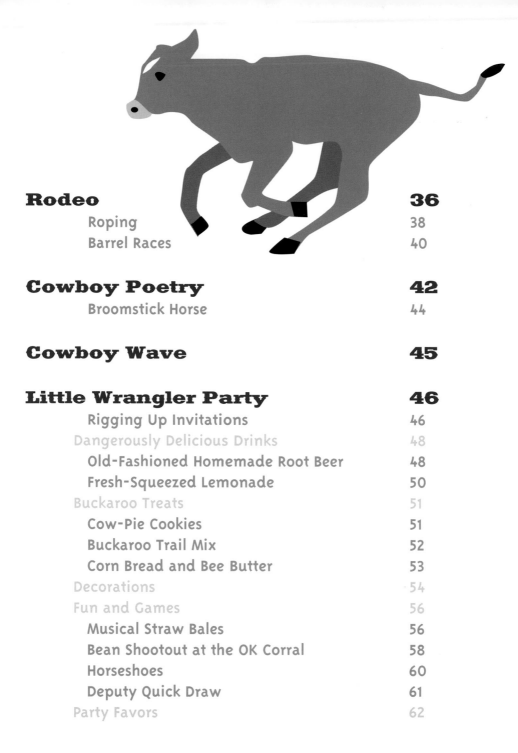

Beans and a Bedroll

A cowboy's job is working cows. Since cows live outside, that's where the cowboy spends most of his time—checking cows, doctoring cows, branding cows, gathering cows, moving cows, or driving cows to market. Sometimes cowboys work by themselves. And sometimes, when moving a whole herd of cows, they work in groups.

Today, in a world that has pickup trucks and four-wheelers, it's not too often that a cowboy has to spend the night outdoors as part of his job. But in days past, a cowboy could be on the trail for weeks without an indoor bed or a hot bath. Some would say that was the hardest part of the job, and some would say that was the best part of the job!

Traveling by horseback meant traveling light, so the cowboy didn't usually carry much gear. Camping for the night meant gathering wood,

building a fire, and rolling out a bedroll under the stars. The bedroll was made of a piece of canvas around 15 feet long and 8 feet wide. Inside was rolled a blanket or two. At bedtime, a cowboy would find a flat place on the ground, get between the blankets, and fold himself in the canvas like a burrito to keep out the wind, dew, and rain.

On large cattle drives, the cows outnumbered the cowboys by about 300 to 1. For a large herd of 2,500 to 3,000 cows, there would be 8 to 10 cowboys driving the herd.

A chuck wagon usually rolled along ahead. It was an outdoor kitchen manned by a cook, or "cookie," who prepared food for the whole outfit. Meals consisted of some combination of beans, bacon, beef, biscuits, potatoes, and always coffee.

Though cattle drives are mostly a thing of the past, you can still get the flavor of one in your own backyard. Find an old piece of canvas or a plastic tarp, borrow a couple of blankets from your bed (be sure to ask your folks first!), and make your own bedroll. Get your mom or dad to help you bake up some biscuits and beans. Find a couple of friends to share the fun. Wait for a clear night, and then share some cowboy grub and sleep out under the stars.

Beans in a Bedroll Recipe

Fold up A
Fold in B and C

For each bedroll, you'll need

For the canvas	1 flour tortilla
For the cowboy	2-3 tablespoons refried beans
For the chaps	$\frac{1}{2}$ slice beef jerky split down the middle, or beef lunch meat cut into two thin strips
For the shirt	$\frac{1}{4}$ cup grated cheddar cheese
For the blanket	1-2 tablespoons salsa or chili sauce

What you do

1. Lay the tortilla on the plate and spread beans in the center. Imagine the beans are the cowboy.

2. Place beef strips side by side on half the length of the cowboy, like chaps.

3. Cheddar cheese can be sprinkled over the upper half of the body, like a shirt.

4. Spread salsa or chili sauce over the cowboy like a blanket.

5. Fold in the sides of the tortilla like a canvas bedroll (see diagram).

6. Cover the bedroll with a damp paper towel and heat in a microwave on high for about 35 seconds. *Delicious warm, but can be eaten cold*

Buckaroo Beans 'n' Biscuits

What you need
- 1/2 pound ground beef or sausage
- 1/2 small onion, diced
- 2 small cans baked beans
- 2 fresh tomatoes, diced (optional)
- 1 can refrigerator biscuits

How to prepare
1. Spray a medium-sized baking dish with oil to make cleanup easier.
2. Fry meat with onion in a frying pan until the meat is browned, and set aside.
3. Open beans and pour into the baking dish. Dump meat and tomatoes over the beans and stir until all are mixed together.
4. Crack the can of biscuits open. Arrange pieces of biscuit dough over top of bean mixture. Snuggle them up so all the biscuits fit.
5. Bake at 350 degrees for about 25 minutes. Watch for the biscuits to turn golden. When the biscuits are done, remove the dish from the oven and let cool a little bit before serving.

Cowboy Duds

"**I** see by your outfit that you are a cowboy . . . " begins an old cowboy song. A cowboy's duds, or clothes, are an important part of the job. He wears an outfit to match the work he does. From top to bottom, here's what you'll find most cowboys wearing: a hat, a shirt, cuffs or gauntlets, a bandana, a vest, blue jeans, a belt buckle, chaps, boots, and sometimes spurs.

Cowboy Hat

A cowboy's broad-brimmed hat protects him from the sun, rain, wind, and dust. The size and shape of a cowboy's hat can tell us about the person—such as what part of the country he is from and maybe what kind of work he does. It's kind of like his personal signature. Hats are made with different brim sizes, crown heights, and creases. Some popular styles are a cattleman's crease, the buckaroo style, and the Tom Mix (named after a hero of cowboy films in the early 1900s).

Australian Akubra

Mexican Sombrero

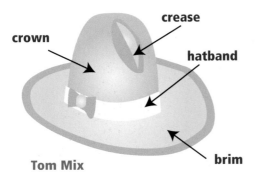

crown

crease

hatband

brim

Tom Mix

Plainsman

Ten Gallon

Modern-day Stetson

Cowboy Manners

Cowboy manners say that a cowboy may leave his hat on almost all the time, even when he's inside someone's house. In fact, a working cowboy almost never takes off his hat. An old saying is that his hat is the first thing a cowboy puts on in the morning, and the last thing he takes off at night.

Shirt

Cowboys almost always wear long-sleeved shirts—even in very hot weather. That is because their shirts protect them from the sun, wind, insect bites, and scratches from thistles or barbed wire. Sometimes you'll see younger ones in T-shirts, but the old buckaroos won't be caught that way. In western horse show events and at the rodeo, riders are required to wear western attire, which includes a long-sleeved shirt. Cowboy shirts are usually made of cotton or denim and often have darts in the front for a snug fit. Since the 1940s, traditional cowboy shirts have been made with pearl-snap buttons. That's changing a bit now, but many cowboys still like the traditional pearl-snap look.

Vest

A cowboy's vest is made of leather, wool, or canvas. It provides extra pockets for carrying things, or extra insulation when it's cold outside. Vests are also a matter of cowboy style. They can be plain and made of canvas, or fancy with leather fringe. Cowgirls wear vests too—both for working and for dressing up.

Make Your Own Cowboy Vest

What you need

> **Basics: paper grocery bag, pencil, scissors**
>
> **Extras: markers, paints, colored construction paper, glue, glitter, fabric, or cord**

Directions

1. Lay your grocery bag flat and trace out a design for your vest with your pencil.
2. Cut out your vest, being careful to make an opening only in the front.
3. Color or decorate your vest.

Blue Jeans

The standard pants worn by working cowboys today are blue jeans. They are worn on the ranch, in the saddle, and even at cowboy weddings!

The original blue jeans were invented by a man named Levi Strauss, who made and sold them to miners during the California gold rush of 1849. His company still exists, and you may even own a pair of Levi's jeans.

Many of today's cowboys prefer another brand of jeans called Wrangler. They are made with a little extra room in the seat and leg for comfort while on horseback, and the legs of the jeans fit over the tops of cowboy boots. These jeans are longer than normal pants so that the tops of a cowboy's boots remain covered when he is on his horse with his knees bent. When a cowboy stands up, his jeans hang down below his boots, causing the bottom edge of the pants to become worn and frayed in the back.

Bandanas, Scarves, and Wild Rags

Early cowboy shirts were made without collars, so cowboys started using square pieces of cloth, usually two feet across, called bandanas, scarves, or wild rags. The cowboys tied these bandanas around their necks to protect them from the elements. Traditional bandana colors are red or blue, but sometimes other solid colors or even prints are used. They can be made of cotton, but are much more comfortable if they are made of silk.

Cowboys tie their bandanas different ways, depending on what they are doing.

On a cattle drive   Working in the sun   At a dance

The Bandana's Many Uses

In addition to sun and wind protection around a cowboy's neck, a bandana can be used as a dust mask, a handkerchief, a bandage, a sling, a washcloth, a towel, a tourniquet, a napkin, a potholder, a signaling flag, or to put medicine on a horse. It can also be used to filter cowboy coffee or strain silt out of creek water. In the old western movies, the bad guys used a bandana to hide their identity when robbing a bank or a train. How many more uses can you think of for a bandana?

Cool Bandana Pillow

Materials needed

    2 bandanas,
    same size, any color

    1 yard of thread in a color
    that matches bandanas

    1 skein embroidery thread in a
    color that contrasts with bandanas

    Needle

    Stuffing (old clean pantyhose,
    leftover quilt batting, or 2 bags
    of cotton balls)

    One pair 12-inch leather shoelaces

running stitch

adjacent sides

whipstitch

Directions

1. Lay two bandanas on floor with right sides together.

2. Stitch one side of the layered bandanas together with a running stitch. Make a $^3/_8$-inch seam.

3. Stitch the two adjacent sides together, and leave a 5-inch opening in the middle of the last side.

4. Turn the pillowcase right side out. Pull the corners out so they are square.

5. Stuff two cotton balls into each corner. Then stuff pillowcase.

6. Fold under both open edges and pin them together. Stitch the opening closed.

7. Decorate pillow edges with embroidery thread. Using a double thread, whipstitch over the seams along the outside edge of the pillow.

8. Cut each shoelace in half. Gather each corner of the pillowcase and tie with a piece of leather.

Boots

A cowboy's boots are just as important as his hat. A good pair of handmade boots is expensive, and a cowboy can expect to pay a month's wages (or more) for them. Some cowboy boots are designed with high heels so that his foot doesn't accidentally get hung up in the stirrup of the saddle. Pointed toes make it easy to slip their boots into a stirrup.

Most working cowboys wear their jeans hanging over their boots, but some prefer to tuck their jeans into their boots. This is called "shotgun" style.

Belts and Buckles

Sometimes you'll know a cowboy by his belt, because he'll have his name or initials carved into the back of it. These belts are usually made of leather and are about 1 to 2 inches wide. They can be decorated with rawhide, beads, carving, or silver. A belt does more than hold up pants. It is a decorative item that reflects the cowboy's personality. It also provides a way to show off those big silver belt buckles that are a part of the costume. Many cowboy competitions (like rodeos and horse shows) give belt buckles for prizes, and cowboys wear them proudly. A rule of thumb in the cowboy world is **"the bigger the buckle, the better."**

Make Your Own Belt Buckle

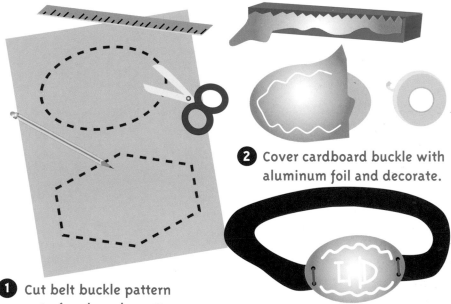

2 Cover cardboard buckle with aluminum foil and decorate.

1 Cut belt buckle pattern out of carboard, any shape you want.

3 Punch holes on sides of buckle and attach to your own belt with string or rubber bands.

Chaps

Chaps (pronounced "shaps") are seatless protective leggings made of cowhide and worn over the front and side of the cowboy's jeans. (The word *chaps* is shorthand for the Spanish word *chaparajos,* meaning "leather overalls.") They protect the rider from cold, rain, sun, and from scrapes and scratches caused by riding through the brush in search of a lost cow, or from the occasional horse that wants to take a bite out of a leg.

Chaps are made in four basic styles with dozens of variations to each pattern.

1	2	3	4
Shotguns	Woolies	Batwings	Chincs

1. **Shotguns are made with leg holes that look like shotgun barrels and wrap all the way around the legs.**

2. **Woolies are like shotguns but are made out of warm fur from an animal such as beaver, bear, or buffalo.**

3. **Batwings fasten in the rear and have large flaps on the sides that resemble wings. These, the fanciest of all chaps, can be decorated with leather fringe and silver conchos (like buttons, with etched decoration). This is the style usually preferred by rodeo cowboys.**

4. **Chincs fall just below the knee.**

Make Your Own Chaps

Materials

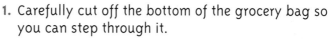

1 paper grocery bag, large enough to step into (a bag without writing is best)

Markers or crayons

Beads or buttons and glue (optional)

Scissors

Twine

Scotch tape

Directions

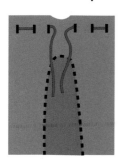

1. Carefully cut off the bottom of the grocery bag so you can step through it.

2. Step into the grocery bag. Have an adult mark the front of the bag to show where to make the leg openings for your chaps.

3. Carefully step out of the grocery bag. Cut the two leg openings with scissors. Since chaps are worn over a cowboy's jeans, the back is seatless. Cut a deeper opening on the back.

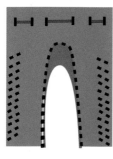

4. For a twine belt, cut about a dozen small slits all around the grocery bag, about 1 to 2 inches from the top. You may want to reinforce the slits with pieces of tape.

5. Cut a piece of twine long enough to fit around your waist, plus about 12 inches more. Thread the twine in and out of the slits. Tie the two ends of the twine together in front, adjusting for comfort.

6. For fringe, cut short strips of the grocery bag on the legs of the chaps. Ruffle them so the fringe stands out.

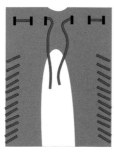

7. Decorate your chaps. Some ideas: diamond shapes; decorative circles with letters inside them, such as RR for Double R Ranch; a colorful border; or shiny dots that look like beads. You may also decorate your chaps with beads or buttons. Chaps have small pockets. Draw and decorate these, too.

Cuffs or Gauntlets

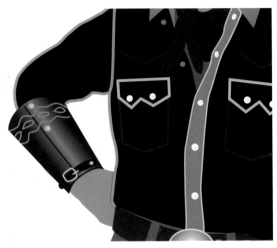

Cowboys wear leather cuffs, or gauntlets, to protect their wrists and arms from hot branding irons, the end of a steer's horns, or brush and thistles. Sometimes more decorative than useful, cuffs are frequently made of tooled leather and decorated with *conchos* (silver buttons with designs).

Make Your Own Gauntlets

Materials
- 1 sheet of plain white paper
- 1 piece of poster board about 6 x 12 inches
- Crayons or markers, pencil for tracing
- 2 pieces of construction paper for fringe, each about 2 inches wide
- Scissors
- Stapler or Scotch tape
- Old gardening gloves (optional)

What to do
1. Trace the gauntlet pattern on a sheet of plain white paper. Cut out the pattern.
2. Trace around the white pattern onto the poster board twice (once for each gauntlet). Cut out the patterns.
3. Using crayons or markers, decorate the outside of both pieces of poster board. You might draw fancy designs such as flowers, horseshoes, or diamonds. Squiggly lines or a small star are other options. You might want to make the cuffs look like they have beads or stitching.
4. Next add fringe to the gauntlets, using construction paper. Cut slits about halfway across, all the way up one long side of each piece of paper.

Enlarge this pattern
for gauntlet 200%.

Bottom (wrist)

5. To make the poster board into cuffs, roll it so it is curved at the bottom a little larger than your wrist. Have someone mark the spot where the top edge fits. Overlap one side of the poster board over the other and tape it. The opening at the bottom should be just big enough to squeeze your hand through.

6. Attach the fringe to the topside of each gauntlet, as shown in the drawing.

7. Put on the old gardening gloves if you wish.

8. Pull on the gauntlets to rest at your wrists. Congratulations! You're ready to brand some cattle and clear some brush.

Spurs

When a real cowboy walks into the room, you will probably hear the "clink" of his spurs. Spurs are attached to the heel of a cowboy's boot and aid the cowboy in guiding his horse. The shank, a piece of metal sticking out from the heel, holds the rowel, which is the part of the spur that comes into contact with the horse. Rowels can have dull edges or sharper points, depending upon the style of the spur. Sometimes a small piece of metal called a "jinglebob" hangs from the center of the rowel. The jinglebob makes a gentle jingling sound when the cowboy moves his feet.

shank rowel

jinglebobs

Besides their practical uses, spurs are also a part of the cowboy's fashion statement. Sometimes the spur is inlaid with gold or silver designs, or with a cowboy's initials.

Books on Cowboy Duds

If you'd like to learn more about cowboy clothes and gear, you'll find a number of books at your local library. Two particularly nice ones are *100 Years of Western Wear* and *The Cowboy Boot Book*, both written by Tyler Beard, with wonderful photographs by Jim Arndt.

Make Your Own Spurs

Materials

2 pieces of 2-inch wide cardboard, each long enough to fit around your ankle

Crayons (brown or black)

Pencil

Aluminum foil

Waxed paper

Scissors

Paper punch

Small piece of cardboard (big enough for cutting two small circles)

4 Goldtone paper fasteners

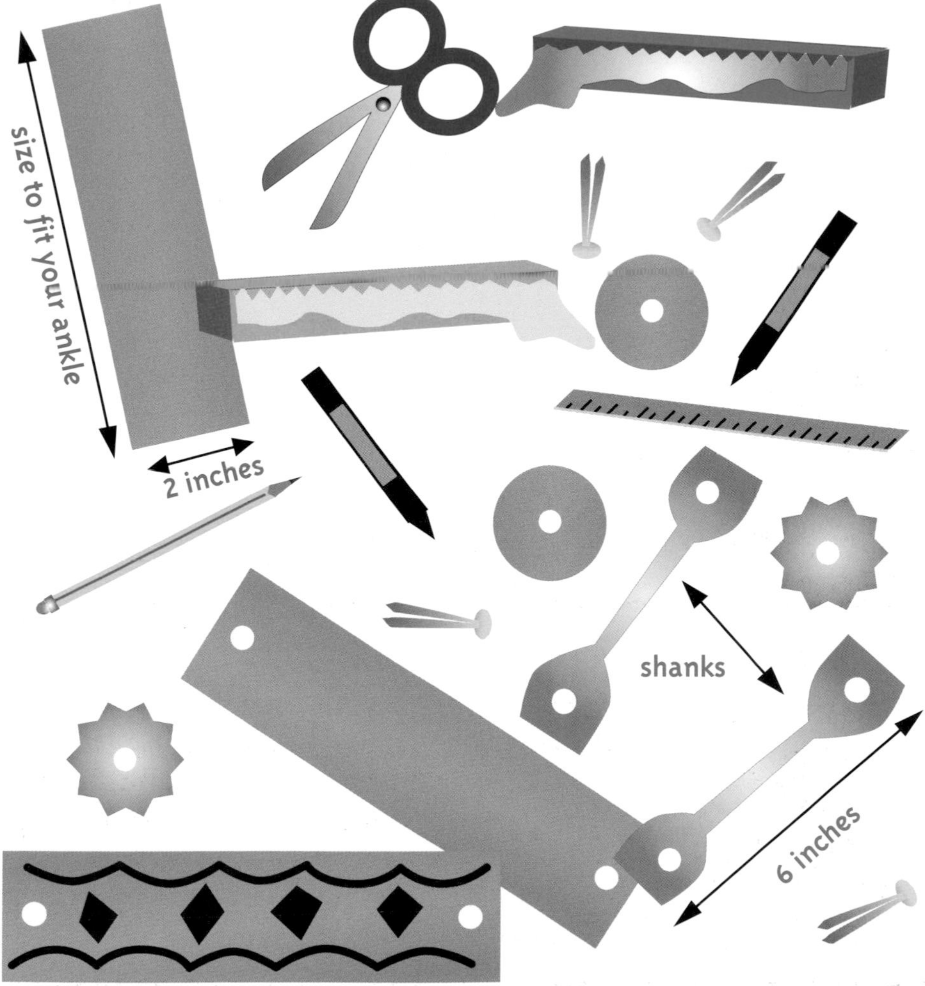

size to fit your ankle

2 inches

shanks

6 inches

1. Color the two pieces of cardboard to make it look like leather.

2. Take a piece of waxed paper and place it anywhere on the cardboard. Draw designs on the waxed paper with a pencil, pressing hard. Do this on both pieces.

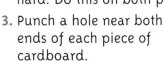
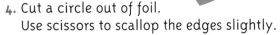

rowel

paper fastener

shank

cardboard circle

3. Punch a hole near both ends of each piece of cardboard.

4. Cut a circle out of foil. Use scissors to scallop the edges slightly.

5. Cut a slightly smaller circle out of cardboard.

6. Put the foil circle over the cardboard circle and use the paper punch to make a hole in both circles. This is the rowel.

7. For the shank, cut a piece of foil about 6 inches long. Fold it lengthwise several times.

8. Punch a hole at one end of the folded-over foil. Match this hole with the holes in the foil and cardboard circles (foil circle, cardboard circle, and foil strip). Use one paper fastener to attach all three.

9. To attach the shank to the cardboard strap, punch a hole about two inches from the other end of the foil strip.

10. Fold the end of the foil so its hole lines up with the hole on the inside of the cardboard strap. Match the hole on the other end of the strap so it's on top of the foil hole. All holes should line up (cardboard, foil, cardboard). Attach the paper fastener to the outside of the cardboard strap; it will hold all three holes together.

11. Crinkle the foil strip so it's skinny and stronger.

Wahoo! You've got spurs!

strap

shank

rowel

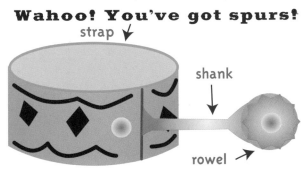

Cowboy Lingo

Just like any other group, cowboys have their own special language. If you hang around the bunkhouse, the rodeo, or anyplace else cowboys gather, you may hear some of these words being used.

boot hill—cemetery

broke—that a horse is gentle and ready to ride

bronc—an unbroken horse, or a horse that, though broke, is still a bit wild

buckaroo—cowboy (from the Spanish word *vaquero*)

bunkhouse—living quarters for the cowboys working on a ranch

calaboose—jail

catch pen—a corral for holding cattle or horses

chow—food

chuck—food

cookie—the cook

corral—fenced-off area for livestock

cowboy up—mount up and ride out, or grin and bear it

critter—cow or other animal

crow hop—a mini-buck; the horse rounds its back and hops

dogie—an orphaned calf

draw—a lottery that matches riders and animals at rodeo events

dude—city slicker

grub—food

hand—a ranch worker

hightail—to run off or get away fast

hoss—horse

hung off—a foot caught in the stirrup of the saddle

maverick—a stray, unbranded calf

mustang—wild horse

outfit—a ranch worker's or a cowboy's pickup truck

pard—partner, friend

ride the line—check the fences to fix any that are broken

rig—saddle

spread—a ranch

stove up—hurt, injured, or crippled cowboy

try—effort ("Bill has a lot of try in him.")

wrangler—the cowboy who takes care of the horses

wreck—a riding accident

Let's Put On a Play!

Use one of these ideas, or come up with your own, to write a play. The actors could use some of the cowboy lingo for their dialogue (the words they speak in the play) to tell a story about cowboys and cowgirls. Here are some ideas to help you get started.

Script Ideas

1. Wranglers Bill and Rusty ride out on the range to look for a lost dogie. They have an adventure.

2. Cowboys and cowgirls perform in a rodeo.

3. Cowboy Hank and his buddies sit around a campfire, eating dinner and singing songs. Suddenly they hear a coyote howl nearby.

4. Something is spooking the herd. Is it a rustler? Could it be a rattle-snake? Cowgirl Sue investigates and solves the problem.

5. City slickers come to a ranch to learn how to be cowboys.

6. Cowboys are playing cards in the bunkhouse when an argument breaks out.

Props

Now let's find props for your play.

For example, if your play is about Cowboy Hank and his buddies around a campfire eating dinner, make a pretend campfire with a bunch of sticks in a pile. (Don't make a real fire!) Maybe around the campfire you can even be eating some of the food made from the cowboy recipes in this book.

If your play is about performing in a rodeo, use a rope to lasso the steer you made (see pages 38–39 for roping and directions on how to make a steer), or use trashcans for barrel racing competition (see pages 40–41). The rope, steer, and trashcans would be your props.

Costumes

See the directions on pages 14 to 26 for making vests, chaps, belts, gauntlets and spurs. Use these and other clothing items to dress up as cowboys and cowgirls in your play.

Music

There are many good cowboy songs, such as *Home on the Range, Happy Trails*, and *I'm An Old Cowhand*. Consider singing a cowboy song as the finale (the very end) to your play. Check your local library, or do a search for "cowboy songs" on the Internet. Your song is sure to generate a lot of applause from the audience!

Branding

In the days of the open range, cattle ran free with no fences to keep them in one place. So that ranchers would know whose cattle belonged to whom (and to keep rustlers from helping themselves), critters were branded, or marked. This was done in the spring shortly after all of the calves had been born.

A brand is the official mark (like a signature) of the ranch to which the brand belongs. Choosing a brand is serious business because the mark stays with a ranch for a long time, frequently being passed on from generation to generation. Brands have to be registered with livestock officials called "brand inspectors" so that more than one ranch doesn't have the same brand. All brands are different and some are quite famous, like the Running W from the *King Ranch* in Texas or the Elkhorn that belonged to Teddy Roosevelt, the twenty-sixth president of the United States.

Running W   Elkhorn

At branding time, cowboys gather the calves, put them in a corral, rope them one at a time, and then vaccinate and brand them. The branding iron is heated in a hot fire or stove in order to sear the mark on the calf's shoulder or hip flesh. The calf is sore for a couple of days, but the brand soon heals over. Once a brand is properly done, it stays with the animal forever.

Real branding is NOT something you should try at home, but you can dream of registering your own brand someday. Why not design a brand of your own?

As you think of what it might look like, remember these simple rules—brands are read left to right, top to bottom, and outside to inside.

Here are some common ranch symbols (brands):

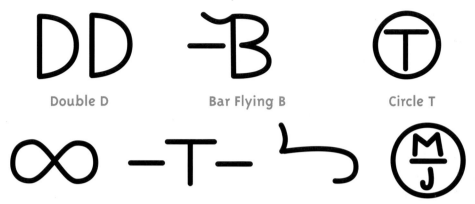

Double D   Bar Flying B   Circle T

Lazy 8   Bar T Bar   Lazy Flying J   Circle M Bar J

A number or letter lying on its side is LAZY, and — means BAR. A tail on a letter means "flying." The way symbols are combined tells the name of the ranch.

Can you guess the names of these funny brands?

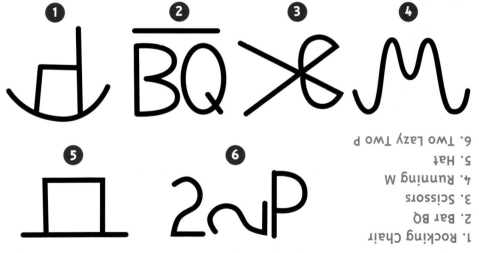

1. Rocking Chair
2. Bar BQ
3. Scissors
4. Running M
5. Hat
6. Two Lazy Two P

Get some paper and a pencil and work on your own brand design. See if you can get it to tell a story or make a word picture like the Lazy 8 or the Running W.

Carving Your Brand

After you design your brand, there is a way you can see what it might look like if it were actually made and used. Get permission from an adult first.

What You Need

Your brand design

1 raw baking potato (will make 2 brands)

Waterproof felt marker, pencil or toothpick

Paring knife (ask for adult help)

Inked stamp pad

Paper bag or old T-shirt

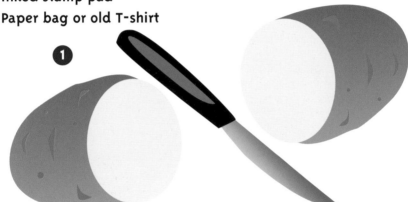

Directions

1. Cut potato cleanly in half so you end up with two smooth surfaces. This will make 2 brands.

2. Use a waterproof felt marker, a pencil, or a toothpick to draw your brand on the cut surface of the potato.

3. With a paring knife, carefully cut away about ½ inch of the potato around your brand. When you have finished, your very own brand will stand out. This is your "branding iron"!

4. Use the inked stamp pad to rub some ink onto your brand.

5. Brand a paper bag and cut out a section for a sign to hang on your bedroom door. Or brand an old T-shirt (be sure to ask your mom first) and wear it proudly. Please don't brand your dog or your little sister! Your potato is perishable, so it won't last forever. When it starts to shrivel, just carve yourself another brand.

My brand is called the *Happy Star!*

33

One of the ways cowboys used brands was on signs for their ranches. You can make your own ranch sign with an old piece of wood or a piece of sturdy cardboard. Glue twigs to your sign to form your brand or paint your brand on it. Hang your sign on the door to your room, clubhouse, or fort.

The Branding Game

The Circle Rocking T!

1. Play this game with two teams.
2. Each team makes up ten brands and draws them clearly on ten notecards or pieces of writing paper. (Don't let the other team see your brands yet!)
3. Decide which team will "present" first. Set a timer for 5 minutes. The presenter shows one card at a time while the opposing team guesses the name of each brand.
4. The guessing team may either try to guess the name of the brand or say "pass" if they are wasting too much time with wrong answers.
5. When they have either guessed it correctly or said "pass," the presenter quickly moves to the next card.
6. When the 5-minute buzzer rings, score 5 points for each right answer, and record the team's score.
7. Switch places so the presenting team becomes the guessing team.
8. At the end of one round, the team with the highest number of points wins. You may complete additional rounds of the game as long as your group wants to continue playing.

Rodeo

Rodeo is an exciting and popular sport that originated from everyday jobs done by cowboys on the ranch and on the range. Cows (females), calves (youngsters), and steers (neutered males) were roped to doctor or to brand. Young horses were ridden through their "bucking" stage as they progressed toward being trained as working stock. Eventually cowboys made a game of these activities by seeing how long they could stay on the back of a bucking horse or how fast they could rope and tie a calf.

Today's organized rodeo includes the following events:

Bareback Riding

While holding on with only one hand, a cowboy tries to ride a wildly bucking bronco and stay on for at least eight seconds.

Calf Roping

Riding on horseback at full speed, a cowboy ropes a calf, jumps off his horse, and ties the legs of the calf together in the fastest possible time.

Bulldogging or Steer Wrestling

At full speed on horseback, a cowboy chases a running steer. He jumps from his horse, grabs the steer by its horns, and wrestles it to the ground as quickly as possible.

Saddle Bronc Riding

This is similar to bareback riding, except during this event the horse has a saddle on its back.

Barrel Racing

One of the speediest events in rodeo, cowgirls on fast horses race around three barrels in the rodeo arena. The rider with the best time wins.

Team Roping

Two cowboys or cowgirls on horseback race after a running steer. One rider (called a header) ropes the head of the steer, and the other rider (called a heeler) ropes the hind legs, in the fastest possible time.

Bull Riding

This is the most dangerous event in rodeo. Cowboys try to ride on twisting, twirling, bucking bulls for eight seconds.

If you are interested in seeing a rodeo, one may come to a fairground or arena near you. Keep your eyes on the newspaper or ask someone at your local tack or feed store. If you would like to find out more about professional rodeo, you can go to www.prorodeo.com.

Even if you don't go to a real rodeo, there are a couple of rodeo-like events you might want to try in your own neighborhood. They don't require real horses or cattle, but you will need to make or find a couple of things around your house before you get started.

Roping

For this activity, you'll need a lasso and something to catch. If you are lucky enough to know a rancher or working cowboy, they may have an old lariat or lasso that they might be willing to give you. If not, you can make one out of a piece of rope or cotton clothesline about 20 feet long.

1. Tie a tight loop in one end of your rope, thread the other end of the rope through that loop to make a big loop. Now you are ready to rope and ride!

2. As for something to rope, DO NOT practice on anything living, including your dog, your cat, or your little brother or sister! Ropes can be deadly if misused. Instead, build yourself a roping steer. If you have an adult helper who is a woodworker, get him or her to cut a steer head out of a

piece of plywood or shelving board. Or you could make one out of heavy cardboard.

3. Attach your steer head to a bale of hay or straw, a sawhorse, or a heavy-duty cardboard box. You have built a roping steer! Even real cowboys sometimes practice on homemade steers.

4. Practice coiling your rope by holding the end with the loop in one hand and looping the rest of the rope in wide loops around the other hand. Get a good grip on the loose rope end. Swing your rope in a circle over your head and throw it over the horns of your steer. Start out at close range and as you get the hang of throwing the loop, move farther and farther away. You can make a game of roping by seeing how many times in a row you can rope the steer, or by timing how fast you can rope it five times.

Barrel Races

Barrel Racing Pattern

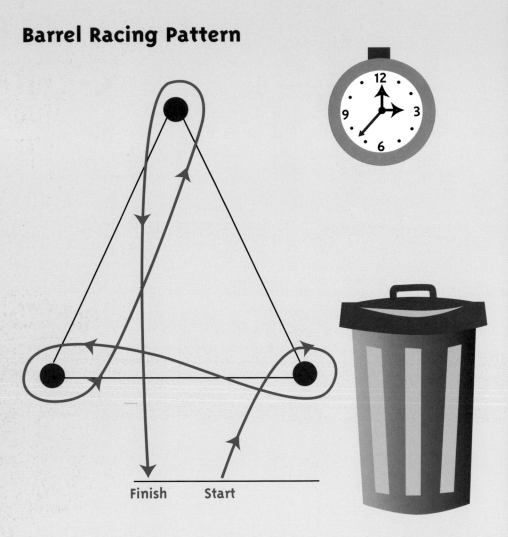

Finish   Start

Gather some of your friends and stage a barrel racing rodeo event without horses.

1. Get three empty trash cans to use as barrels. Set them up in your yard as they would be in a real rodeo.

2. Mark a starting line with a piece of rope or a stick and find a watch that shows minutes and seconds.

3. Then run the barrel pattern just like you would if you were on horse-back. Have someone time your run and record it. Make sure everyone in the group has a turn.

4. The person with the best time wins.

5. If anyone knocks over a barrel while running around it, his or her time should be penalized by five seconds.

Cowboy Poetry

owboys and cowgirls spend a lot of time in the outdoors. Their kitchen is the campfire, their bedroom is the meadow by a stream, and their alarm clock is the sun sneaking up over the hills to the east. There is something about this way of life that causes folks to want to express themselves in verse and rhyme that we call "cowboy poetry."

Most of the time, cowboys were a long way from any form of entertainment, so they made up verses and recited them to one another as a way of passing the time in the evenings. These poems tell the stories of a cowboy's life. They talk about the weather, the land, the cattle, and the horses that make up the center of their lives. Sometimes they talk about love or loneliness. Often they are funny, and occasionally they are sad. Always they speak of cowboy traditions and the cowboy way of life.

Frequently, but not always, cowboy poems are written in four-line stanzas, with the last word in the second and fourth lines rhyming—like this:

The cowboy and his horse were headin'
Straight toward the steer.
The horse stopped short, the man fell off
And nearly broke his . . . ear.

There are many, many cowboy poets. A few, like Baxter Black, Wally McRae, and Waddie Mitchell, have become famous for their work. You can find collections of cowboy poetry in the library. One that is especially nice is *Cowboy Poetry: A Gathering.*

Now that you have learned a little about the cowboy way of life, why don't you try your hand at writing a poem or two? Here is a list of rhyming words that you can use to help get you started:

rope — lope — hope — mope — soap
brand — hand — land — sand — band
cow — how — now — plow
gun — run — fun — sun
tall — fall — bawl — brawl — crawl — ball — small — hall — call
town — down — round — found — sundown — mound
ride — hide — glide — slide — guide — tried
road — load — toad
night — tight — fight — light — height — sight — bright — starlight — might
trot — hot — not — plot
tail — wail — hail — trail — sail — nail — fail — pail — mail
boss — hoss — loss — toss
deal — squeal — wheel — meal — feel
grass — pass — lass — class
boot — shoot — toot — hoot
string — ring — sing — thing
stock — flock — clock — knock
beans — jeans — mean — clean
cattle — saddle — skedaddle

Here are some other subject words to help you along:

sunset	**hills**	**prairie**
dusty	**valley**	**range**
lonesome	**roundup**	**rodeo**
wind	**buckaroo**	**horses**

All you need now is a pencil, paper, and a quiet place to think. You'll be a poet before you know it! Have your friends write poems too, and then put on a cowboy poetry gathering to entertain your neighborhood. Everyone can wear their cowboy duds, tie on a bandana in their favorite way, and perform their poems for a live audience! If you're really adventuresome, you can serve up a mess of Beans in a Bedroll or Buckaroo Beans 'n' Biscuits.

Broomstick Horse

Materials
big old sock
broomstick
quilt batting
felt
buttons
needle and thread

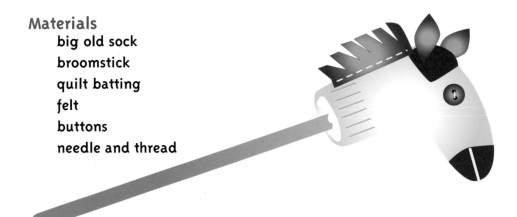

1. Stuff a big old sock with quilt batting or anything else you want.
2. Push it onto a broomstick or other stick that's about the length of horse you want.
3. Cut out pieces of felt or sew on buttons for eyes.
4. Cut out ears from felt and put those on with hot glue or stitch them on.
5. Make slits in a strip of 6-inch wide felt and sew that on for a mane. Easy as cowpies, right?

Cowboy Wave

After his horse, the favorite mode of transportation for any cowboy is a pickup truck. When they are behind the steering wheel, cowboys share one habit that shows a friendly community spirit. It's the "cowboy wave."

Cowboys always wave to folks in passing vehicles—whether they know them or not. It's not a big, flashy, full-handed "howdy-do?" kind of wave, but instead a friendly, low-key recognition of a passing friend or stranger. The cowboy wave is usually done by the driver, but since you are probably not of driving age yet, you can practice it from the passenger side of your car.

The wave is one-handed and is done without taking the hand off the steering wheel. Every cowboy has his own style and uses his same wave all of the time. Some lift just an index finger, some the first two fingers, some raise all four fingers, and some four fingers and the thumb. (Lifting your second and third fingers without lifting your thumb or pinky finger is really hard—try it!)

Now, you might think the cowboy wave is no big deal, but if you stop to consider it for a moment it makes good sense. This simple little wave says to another person, "Hello—I noticed you today." It's a small act of kindness that doesn't cost a thing, and the world can use more gestures like that.

So, start practicing now for the day you'll be driving your own pickup truck. Then you'll already have your perfect cowboy wave.

Little Wrangler Party

Yee-haw! The West is known for tall tales, and nothin' will be as tall as the tales your friends will be tellin' everyone once they attend your Little Wrangler Party.

Rigging up Invitations

For this western-themed party, you should send out invitations at least two weeks in advance. Make your invitation look like an old-fashioned "Wanted" poster that a pony express rider would deliver.

Make the poster out of brown construction paper or a paper bag. Cut out letters for **WANTED** from magazines or newspapers and paste them onto the poster.

FRIENDS TO HAVE FUN AT
LITTLE WRANGLER
PARTY!
When: Saturday, May 12
Time: 3:00pm
Where: Lawson's Corral
123 South St.

Please wear western duds.

Then handwrite the details. Be sure to include the following information:

What: Little Wrangler Western Party
When: Date and time of your party
Where: Address of your corral

You may also want to put other information, like RSVP (cowboy French for "please reply"), "please wear western duds" or "please, no gifts."

Once you have the invitations looking the way you want, roll them up and tie them with a one-inch-wide strip of bandana fabric. Now they are ready to be delivered. You can even deliver them via pony express by decorating a paper sack to make it look like a mailbag. Dress up like a pony express rider, use your own stick horse (see page 44), your bike, scooter, or skateboard—and you are on your way.

Once the invitations are out, it is time to plan the party.

THE PONY EXPRESS

Before there was a post office or telephones, there was the pony express. This was the fastest way that letters could be delivered from East to West before the advent of trains and cars. The pony express lasted only eighteen months, but it was legendary.

Wiry young men were hired to ride horseback over 1,800 miles in a relay team. They carried letters in a leather pouch flung over their horses' backs. There was only one route, and it ran from St. Joseph, Missouri, to Sacramento, California. At frequent stops along the way (every five to ten miles), riders would switch horses, and at some points new riders would take over. This way, the horses didn't get worn out and could gallop again on another day. At pony express stops, letters would be dropped off, and then carried by coach or horseback rider to their final destinations.

Old-Fashioned Homemade Root Beer

Makes 2¹/₂ gallons! (That's enough for 25 little wranglers.)

Supplies

- 5-gallon water container with spigot—metal or plastic, with a lid
- ¹/₂ bottle root beer extract
- 2¹/₂ pounds sugar
- 1 gallon water + 1¹/₂ gallons water
- 2 to 3 pounds dry ice (buy at the supermarket)
- Long stirring stick or long-handled spoon
- Clean cotton or gardener's gloves for handling dry ice

Directions

1. Pour ¹/₂ bottle of root beer extract into a 5-gallon water container.

2. Add sugar and 1 gallon water. Stir until sugar is dissolved.

3. Add 1¹/₂ gallons more water.

4. Put on gloves and carefully drop in the dry ice. Root beer will begin to boil and smoke. This is how the fizz gets into the root beer. Set the lid on the container loosely, leaving air space for gas to escape. Allow to bubble 1 to 3 hours, until the bubbling has nearly stopped. Stir every 20 minutes to half-hour during the process.

5. Serve cold. There's nothing like homemade root beer to quench the thirsty sweet tooth of wranglers after a day's branding or fence mending.

DRY ICE

Watching root beer bubble and boil is a lot of fun. But dry ice is dangerous! Be extremely careful not to let it touch your skin. Dry ice is so cold it burns! Let the ranch foreman or one of your parents do the handling. And real cowboys don't try sticking their heads in the gas cloud to breathe it. The gas will make you cough and can burn your lungs.

Fresh-Squeezed Lemonade

Makes 2 quarts

Supplies

- 8 large lemons
- 1 cup sugar
- 12-15 ice cubes
- Water
- Mint leaves for decoration
- Two-quart pitcher

Directions

1. Squeeze juice from all the lemons. Measure 1¼ cups juice into a saucepan.

2. Add 1 cup sugar. Turn heat to low. Stay near the stove and stir every minute until the sugar is dissolved.

3. Turn off the stove and remove pan from heat. Allow juice to cool.

4. Pour all the juice into the pitcher. Add 12-15 ice cubes. Fill to the top with water. Stir.

5. Pour into glasses and float a fresh mint leaf in each glass. Fresh lemonade is a favorite of both cowgirls and cowboys.

A COWGIRL SECRET

A cowgirl secret is to roll the whole lemon on the counter, pushing on it with your hands. This softens the inside and makes it easier to get the juice out. Then cut the lemon in half. Squeeze over a bowl to catch the juice. If the ranch cook has a juicer, use that. Otherwise, twist each lemon half over the head of a tablespoon. Work the lemon until you have as much juice out as you can get. Strain or spoon the seeds out of the juice and discard.

Buckaroo Treats
Cow-Pie Cookies

Makes about 2 dozen cookies— no baking needed

Supplies

Medium saucepan

Large cookie sheet covered with waxed paper

Stirring spoon

Cooking spray

1 stick butter

$\frac{1}{4}$ cup cocoa

2 cups sugar

3 tablespoons chunky peanut butter

$\frac{1}{2}$ (10-ounce) can condensed milk

2 teaspoons vanilla extract

3 cups old-fashioned oatmeal

1. Melt butter together with cocoa on medium heat in a saucepan, stirring every 30 seconds.

2. Add sugar and stir until dissolved.

3. Add peanut butter and condensed milk. Turn heat to medium high and bring to boil, stirring constantly so chocolate doesn't burn.

4. As soon as the chocolate mixture boils, remove pan from heat and turn off stove.

5. Add vanilla to chocolate and stir.

6. Then add oatmeal and stir until all the oats are covered with chocolate.

7. Drop cookie mixture by tablespoons onto the cookie sheet. Allow to set for 1 hour before peeling cookies away from the waxed paper.

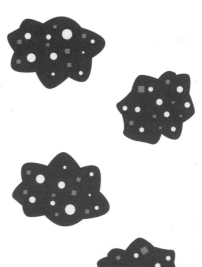

Buckaroo Trail Mix

Makes 4 cups

Mix ½ cup of each of the following ingredients in a plastic bag or bowl with a lid:

Dry roasted peanuts

Candy-coated chocolate pieces

Butterscotch chips

Almonds (whole, sliced, or slivered)

Pretzel sticks

Raisins or craisins

Corn waffle cereal

Graham cereal

Seal and then shake the bag or bowl to toss the mix. Eat by the handful when you're ridin' the trail with your horse and buckaroo buddies.

Corn Bread and Bee Butter

Makes one pie tin

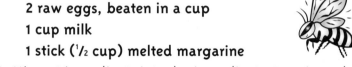

Corn bread

- **2 cups Bisquick**
- **¹/₂ cup sugar**
- **¹/₂ cup yellow cornmeal**
- **¹/₂ teaspoon baking powder**

Stir all these dry ingredients together in a medium-sized bowl.

Add

- **2 raw eggs, beaten in a cup**
- **1 cup milk**
- **1 stick (¹/₂ cup) melted margarine**

1. Mix wet ingredients into dry ingredients. Pour into glass or metal pie plate that has been lightly sprayed with cooking oil.

2. Bake at 350 degrees for 30 minutes, or until top turns golden brown and bread springs back when tapped lightly. Allow to cool for 10 minutes before cutting in wedges, like a pie. Serve with Bee Butter.

Bee Butter

- **1 stick butter or margarine, softened**
- **¹/₄ cup honey**

Stir together with a spoon until well blended.

Decorations

WELCOME to the COW-DOGGY CORRAL

🐄 Make up your own ranch brand and then make a ranch sign to hang in the entranceway to your party corral. (See page 34.)

🐕 Dress up the backyard with bales of straw for chairs.

🐄 Hang pictures of famous cowboys and cowgirls on trees, bushes, straw bales, or wherever you can get them to stick. You can find some to print from your computer at cowboy.com.

🐕 Use pie tins or speckled camping dishes for plates and bandanas for napkins.

🐄 Use a plaid or gingham-checked tablecloth to bring the western look to your tabletop.

Musical Straw Bales

You'll need

A cowboy music CD

A CD player

Bandanas (one for each person at the party)

This game is like playing musical chairs but with straw bales (or whatever you happen to be sitting on at your Little Wrangler Party). Start by choosing a direction of movement (clockwise, counterclockwise, or point out a pony trail if the seats aren't in a formal arrangement).

First, ask everyone to sit down. Be sure everyone has a seat. (Two or three people could share each bale of straw, but you need to be specific about how many people can share a bale.)

Ask everyone to stand up in front of their seat. Now put one bandana on one seat—any seat. The idea is to mark this seat as "out-of-bounds." Once the game begins, no one can sit on that seat. You now have one more person than there are seats.

You'll need a DJ (disc jockey) to start and stop the music. When the music starts, everyone starts walking in the direction you've chosen around the seats. They keep walking until the DJ stops the music.

When that happens, everyone quickly sits down on the nearest seat. But someone isn't going to have a seat, so that person is now an outlaw and has to go to jail. You will want to set up an area that is the jail, maybe marking off a space with a rope.

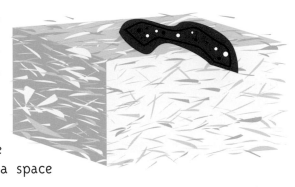

Now mark a second seat with another bandana so there are two seats out-of-bounds. Start the music again. When the music stops, whoever doesn't get a seat is the outlaw—and you know what happens to outlaws!

Continue marking seats out-of-bounds and throwing outlaws into jail until only two people and just one seat remain. Let the music play while the two cowkids jockey for the winning position. The last one sitting is the winner and gets to let everyone out of jail.

Bean Shootout at the OK Corral

AN ADULT RANCH FOREMAN MUST BE ON HAND TO SUPERVISE THE SHOOTOUT!

Materials Needed

    2 wooden clothespins with springs

    Masking tape

    A metal file

    Dry beans for shooting

1. Disassemble both clothespins by twisting the top and bottom to the side so the spring comes loose. Remove the spring.

2. Make a spring notch in one of the clothespin halves. File in the forward curved notch to make a squared corner.

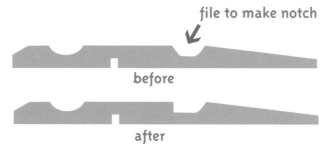

file to make notch

before

after

3. Slide one of the springs onto the notched clothespin half as shown. This becomes the trigger half.

4. Tape the other half of the clothespin to the trigger half.

5. Use one half of the other clothespin to lock the spring in the notch. Push the clothespin into the open "barrel" until the spring slides into the notch.

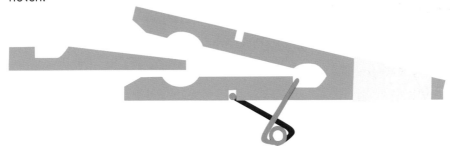

6. SELECT A TARGET FOR PEOPLE TO SHOOT AT. It could be a bulls-eye or a large tin can. Put a dry pea or bean in place and pull back on the trigger to fire. **DO NOT AIM THE BEAN SHOOTER AT ANYONE OR ANY-THING OTHER THAN THE TARGET.**

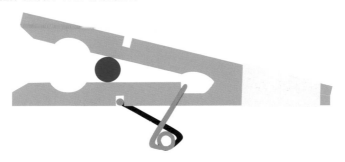

7. Let all the cowkids take turns shooting at the target for several rounds. Whoever hits the target the most times wins.

Horseshoes

Go to a thrift store and find the biggest pair of shoes (horse-sized) you can find.

The game is to see who can toss one shoe the farthest. Have two people out in the corral to mark the landing spot each time a shoe is tossed.

Mark off a starting point in your corral. Everyone has to stand behind the starting point to toss the shoe. If someone's toe goes over the line, that tosser is disqualified. Toss the shoe underhand.

Whoever tosses a shoe the farthest wins!

Deputy Quick Draw

Two teams race against each other to draw a deputy sheriff on paper and then cut him out. The tricky part is that this is a relay race. Each person on the team draws only one piece of the sheriff—an arm, leg, hat, or boots. You can make a list of things the sheriff must include, such as:

Body trunk

Head

Two arms

Two legs

Shirt

Pants

Belt

Vest

Chaps

Boots

Hat

Bolo tie

Star badge

Each team should sit in a circle with a big piece of paper in the middle. After the head cowboy says "go!" the first person should draw one part of the sheriff, then quickly pass the pencil to the person on his left. Keep passing the pencil around the circle until you have drawn the entire sheriff. Now do the same thing to cut out the sheriff from the paper (one part of the sheriff per person). When finished, the last person stands and holds up the sheriff and says, "Deputy Quick Draw at your service!"

Party Favors

Party favors are fun for everyone. Here are some ideas for things to give your guests.

Treats tied up in a bandana

A stick of beef jerky

A couple of pieces of salt water taffy

An apple (for their horses, of course)

Cowboy vests for everyone. You provide the paper bags and decorating supplies. Your friends can make and decorate their own as the final activity at your party before everyone goes home. (See how to make a vest on page 14.)

An autographed picture of you in your cowboy duds.

My Cow-Doggy

My cow-doggy is
black and white.
He follows me around
morning, noon and night.

He's the best little doggy
I ever had.
Always been good,
never been bad.

I love him so much
I tell you it's true.
When I see him comin',
I say Howdy-doo!

An original cowboy poem written by you for this occasion. Decorate the paper with hand-drawn western icons such as hats, boots, coiled ropes, cattle skulls, cactus, Texas stars, and such.

Be sure to take pictures at the party. Everyone will want memories of their special day at your corral.

Collect them all!

Salt Lake City

  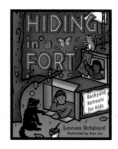

Available at bookstores or directly from
GIBBS SMITH, PUBLISHER
1.800.748.5439/www.gibbs-smith.com